The Illustrated Life & Works of
ROBERT BURNS

COMPILED BY
Alan McNie

CASCADE PUBLISHING COMPANY
Rowandean, Belses, Jedburgh, Scotland

Burns Monument, Alloway.

Contents

Life of Burns *from his correspondence*	3
Funeral of Burns	8
Tam O'Shanter	9
To a Haggis	14
To a Mouse	15
To a Toothache	16
Cotter's Saturday Night	17
John Anderson My Jo	22
Comin Thro' The Rye	23
Scots Wha Hae	24
Flow Gently, Sweet Afton	26
The Banks O' Doon	27
For A' That	28
Auld Lang Syne	29
Burnsiana	30
Acknowledgements	32

Front Cover:

Burns Cottage engraving

Engraving of Burns portrait, after Nasmyth

Engraving of Burns Mausoleum

To Mary, Gregor and Margo

ISBN O 907614 37 X

Alan McNie,

Cascade Publishing Company,

Rowandean, Belses,

Jedburgh, Scotland TD8 6UR.

© 1995 New Edition

Burns Cottage, one of the world's most famous cottages

Written by Rob' Burns
(from correspondence)

Born, at Alloway, near Ayr, 25 January, 1759.

I, was born a very poor man's son. My father, was gardener to a worthy gentleman of small estate. Had he continued in that station, I must have marched off to be one of the little underlings about a farm-house ; but it was his dearest wish and prayer to have it in his power to keep his children under his own eye till they could discern between good and evil.

So with the assistance of his generous master, my father ventured on a small farm on his estate, Mount Oliphant. I made an excellent English scholar ; and by the time I was ten or eleven years of age, I was a critic in substantives, verbs, and particles. In my infant and boyish days too, I owned much to an old woman who resided in the family. She had, I suppose, the largest collection in the country of tales and songs concerning devils, ghosts, fairies, brownies, witches, warlocks, and other trumpery. This cultivated the latent seeds of poetry.

My father's generous master died ; the farm proved a ruinous bargain. We lived very poorly : I was a dextrous ploughman for my age. In my fifteenth autumn, my partner [in harvesting] was a bewitching creature, a year younger than myself. Among her love-inspiring qualities, she sung sweetly, and it was her favourite reel to which I attempted giving an embodied vehicle in rhyme. Thus with me began love and poetry.

My father entered on a larger farm, at Lochlea, about ten miles farther in the country. For four years we loved comfortably here.

(Above) Culzean Castle: Nearby source of fairy stories   (Below): Lochlea

Adapted from Life and Works of Robert Burns, P.H. Waddell (1867)

A difference commencing between my father and his landlord, after three years tossing in the vortex of litigation, my father was just saved from the horrors of a jail by a consumption which, after two years' promises, carried him away.

When my father died, my brother and I took a neighbouring farm at Mossgiel, near Mauchline. But the first year from unfortunately buying bad seed, the second from a later harvest, we lost half our crops.

[Then came] a most melancholy affair [Jean Armour] which I cannot yet bear to reflect on. I gave up my part of the farm to my brother and made what little preparation was in my power for Jamaica.

Before leaving my native country for ever in 1786, I resolved to publish my poems. *Scots Poems chiefly in the Scottish Dialect* printed at Kilmarnock. My vanity was highly gratified by the reception I met with from the public, and besides, I pocketed, all expenses deducted, nearly twenty pounds.

I write this on my tour through a country where savage streams tumble over savage mountains, thinly spread with savage flocks, which starvingly support as savage inhabitants. I had taken the last farewell of my few friends when a letter from Dr. Blacklock to a friend of mine overthrew all my schemes. His opinion that I would meet with encouragement in Edinburgh, for a second edition fired me so much that away I posted to that city. At Edinburgh I was in a new world.

Edinburgh Edition of the *Poems*, sold by William Creech [1787]. I guess I shall clear between two and three hundred pounds by my authorship : with that sum I intend to return to my old acquaintance, the plough.

On seeing a louse on a lady's hat in church:
O wad some Pow'r the Giftie gie us
To see oursels as others see us!

At Dunfermline Abbey, Burns knelt and kissed Bruce's grave.

Above: Burns in Edinburgh by C.M. Hardie. Left to right: Henry Erskine, Dugald Stewart, the Dowager Countess of Glencairn, Adam Ferguson, Robert Burns, Hugh Blair, William Tytler, Henry Mackenzie, William Creech, Alexander Naysmith, Lord Monboddo, the Earl of Glencairn, Margaret Chalmers, Jane, Duchess of Gordon, Miss Burnett, Thomas Blacklock and William Marshall the butler.

An engraver, James Johnson, in Edinburgh, has, not from mercenary views, but from an honest Scotch enthusiasm, set about collecting all of our native songs for The Scots Musical Museum. I have been absolutely crazed about it.

I have married "my Jean" and taken a farm [Ellisland] near Dumfries. With the first step I have every day more and more reason to be satisfied, with the last it is rather the reverse.

I know not how the word, exciseman, or still more opprobrious, gauger, will sound in your ears. I too have seen the day when my auditory nerves would have felt very delicately on this subject ; but a wife and children are things which have a wonderful power in blunting these kind of sensations. Fifty pounds a year for life, and a provision for widows and orphans, you will allow, is no bad settlement for a poet.

Mrs Agnes McLehose left, better known as Clarinda for corresponding purposes with Robert Burns, who was known as Sylvander for the letter-writing liaison. Clarinda, in becoming another female acquaintance, joined a large group from highly disparate backgrounds, apparently fulfilling his many needs.

Burns Tavern, Edinburgh, owned by John Dowie, frequented by Burns

I have sold to my landlord the lease of my farm [Ellisland, 1791].

As to my renumeration, you may think my songs either above or below price ; for they shall absolutely be one or the other.

"The Second Edition" of the *Poems*, "considerably enlarged", 2 vols., Edinburgh. [1793]

A few books which I very much want are all the recompense I crave, together with as many copies of this new edition of my own works as Friendship or Gratitude shall prompt me to present.

Occasional harddrinking is the devil to me. Taverns I have wholly abandoned : it is the private parties in the family way, among the hard drinking gentlemen of this county that do me the mischief – but even this I have more than half given over.

I am on the supervisor' list, [1795] and in two or three years I shall be at the head of that list. The moment I am appointed supervisor I may be nominated on the collectors' list. A collectorship varies much from better than two hundred a year to near a thousand. They have, besides a handsome income a life, of compleat leisure. A life of literary leisure, with a decent competence, is the summit of my wishes.

I fear the voice of the bard will soon be heard among you no more! For these eight or ten months I have been ailing, sometimes bedfast and sometimes not ; but the last three months I have been tortured with excruciating rheumatism which has reduced me to nearly the last stage. What will become of my little flock?   Died at Dumfries, 21 July, 1796.

Brow, place of convalescence

Ellisland, another farming failure, near Dumfries

Spent remaining years of life in Dumfries

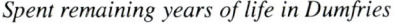

FUNERAL OF ROBERT BURNS

Extract from 22 August, 1796, Edinburgh Courant

But the fact is, that even when all his honours *are* yielded to him, Burns will undoubtedly be found to move in a sphere less splendid, less dignified, and even in his own pastoral stile less attractive than *several* other writers have done; and that poesy was (I appeal to all who had the advantage of being personally acquainted with him) actually *not* his *forte*. If others had climbed more successfully to the heights of Parnassus, *none* certainly ever outshone Burns in the charms— the *sorcery* I would almost call it, of fascinating conversation, the spontaneous eloquence of social argument, or the unstudied poignancy of brilliant repartee. His personal endowments were perfectly correspondent with the qualifications of his mind. His form was manly, his action—energy itself! entirely divested however of all those graces, of that polish, acquired only in the refinement of societies in which *be* seldom had the opportunity to mix ; but *where*, such was the irresistible power of attraction that encircled him, though his manners and appearance were always peculiar, he never failed to delight and to *excel*. His figure certainly bore the authentic impress of his birth and original station in life ; it seemed rather moulded by nature for the rough exercises of agriculture, than the gentler cultivation of the Belles Lettres. His features were stamped with the hardy character of independence, and the firmness of *conscious* though not arrogant pre-emi-

Tribute by Mrs Maria Riddell

Glasgow Mercury, 2nd August, 1796
FUNERAL OF MR. ROBERT BURNS.

Actuated by the regard which is due to the shade of such a genius, his remains were interred on Monday the 25th of July, with military honours and every suitable respect. The corpse, having been previously conveyed to the Town-hall of Dumfries, remained there till the following ceremony took place. The military there, consisting of the Cinque Port Cavalry and the Angusshire Fencibles, having handsomely tendered their services, lined the streets on both sides to the burial ground; the Royal Dumfries Volunteers, of which he was a member, in uniform, with crapes on their left arms, supported the bier ; a party of that corps, appointed to perform the military obsequies, moving in slow solemn time to the Dead March in Saul, which was played by the military band, preceded in mournful array with arms reversed ; the principal part of the inhabitants of that town and neighbourhood, with a number of the particular friends of the bard from remote parts, followed in procession, the great bells of the churches tolling at intervals.

nence. I believe no man was ever gifted with a larger portion of the "*vivida vis animi*" The animated expressions of his countenance were almost peculiar to himself. The rapid lightnings of his eye were always the harbingers of some flash of genius, whether they darted the fiery glances of insulted and indignant superiority, or beamed with the impassioned sentiment of fervent and impetuous affections. His voice alone could improve upon the magic of his eye ; sonorous, replete with the finest modulations, it alternately captivated the ear with the melody of poetic numbers, the perspicuity of nervous reasoning, or the ardent sallies of enthusiastic patriotism. The keenness of satire was, I am almost at a loss whether to say his *forte* or his *foible*: for though nature had endowed him with a portion of the most pointed excellence in that " perilous gift," he suffered it too often to be the vehicle of personal, and sometimes unfounded, animosities.

Mrs Riddell was ideally situated to provide an accurate assessment of Burns. Highly intelligent and strikingly beautiful, this acquaintance, without romantic attachment, 'stretched' Burns as much as anyone.

Tam o' Shanter Inn (Now a museum)

Tam O'Shanter

Poems by Rob¹ Burns

*Or catch'd wi' warlocks in the mirk,
By Alloway's auld haunted kirk.*

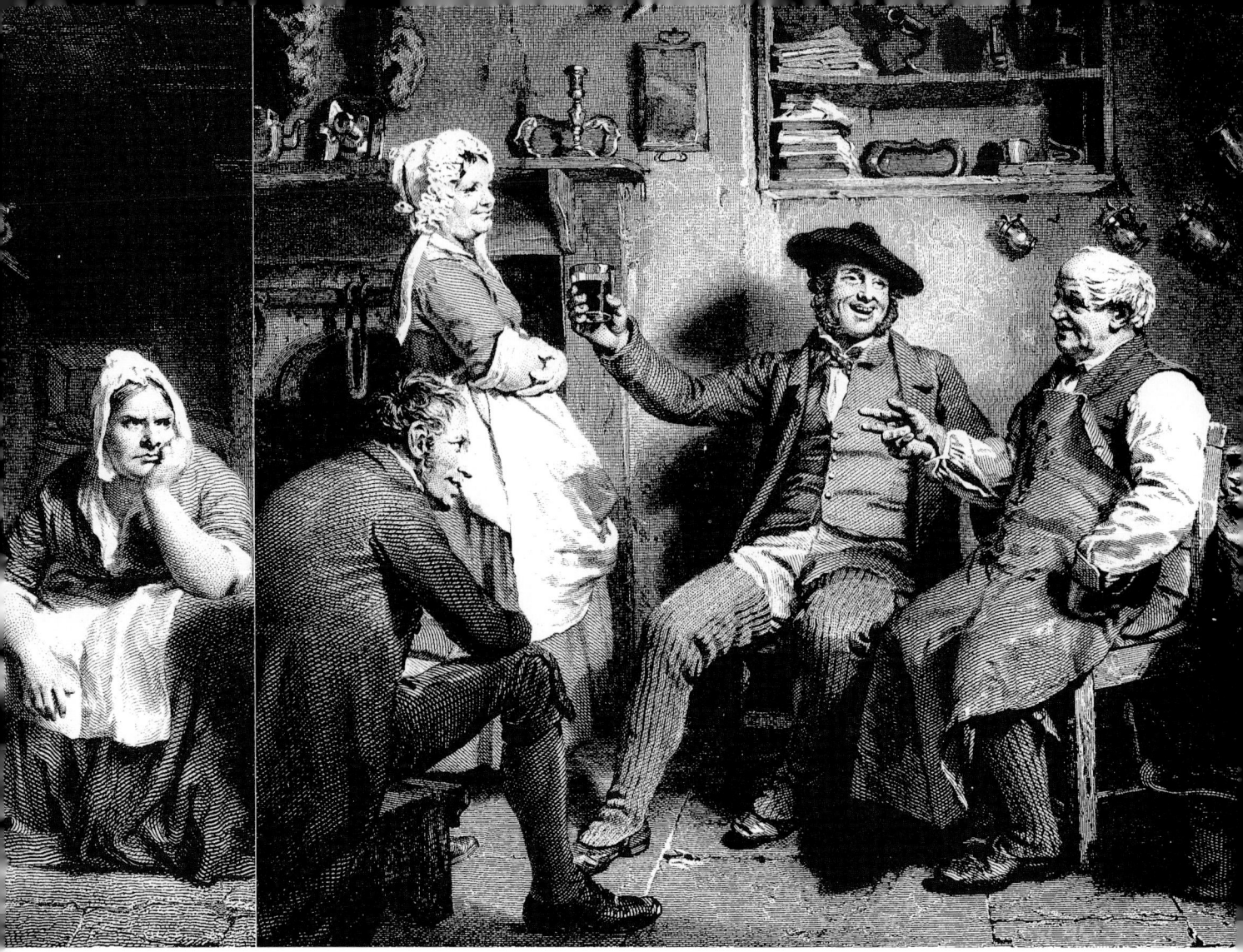

Gathering her brows like gathering storm,
Nursing her wrath to keep it warm.

And at his elbow, Souter Johnny,
His ancient, trusty, drouthy crony

TAM O' SHANTER
A TALE
Of Brownyis and of Bogillis full is this buke.
GAWIN DOUGLAS

packman fellows	WHEN chapman billies leave the street,
thirsty	And drouthy neebors, neebors meet,
	As market-days are wearing late,
road	An' folk begin to tak the gate ;
ale	While we sit bousing at the nappy,
drunk ; very	An' getting fou and unco happy,
not	We think na on the lang Scots miles,
gaps in walls	The mosses, waters, slaps, and styles,
	That lie between us and our hame,
	Whare sits our sulky sullen dame,
	Gathering her brows like gathering storm,
	Nursing her wrath to keep it warm.
found	This truth fand honest Tam o' Shanter,
	As he frae Ayr ae night did canter,
	(Auld Ayr, wham ne'er a town surpasses,
	For honest men and bonny lasses).

	O Tam ! had'st thou but been sae wise,
taken ; own	As ta'en thy ain wife Kate's advice !
rogue	She tauld thee weel thou was a skellum,
chattering babbler	A blethering, blustering, drunken blellum ;
	That frae November till October,
at every meal-grinding	Ae market-day thou was nae sober
	That ilka melder, wi' the miller,
money	Thou sat as lang as thou had siller ;
nag that had a shoe driven on	That ev'ry naig was ca'd a shoe on,
	The smith and thee gat roaring fou on ;
	That at the Lord's house, even on Sunday,
	Thou drank wi' Kirkton Jean till Monday.
	She prophesied that, late or soon,
	Thou would be found deep drown'd in Doon ;
wizards ; darkness	Or catch'd wi' warlocks in the mirk,
	By Alloway's auld haunted kirk.
makes ; weep	Ah, gentle dames ! it gars me greet,
	To think how mony counsels sweet,
	How mony lengthen'd sage advices,
	The husband frae the wife despises !

Regarded by Burns as his best work, Tam o' Shanter is also considered by some authorities as one of the best, if not the best, narrative poem in the English language. This rollicking tale has a background of Alloway locations, not forgetting a daunting array of warlocks, witches and local characters, with Burns undoubtedly drawing on stories he was told as a young child at his first homes.

But to our tale : Ae market-night,
Tam had got planted unco right ;
Fast by an ingle, bleezing finely,   *frothing ale*
Wi' reaming swats, that drank divinely ;
And at his elbow, Souter Johnny,   *Cobbler*
His ancient, trusty, drouthy crony ;
Tam lo'ed him like a vera brither ;
They had been fou for weeks thegither.
The night drave on wi' sangs and clatter ;
And ay the ale was growing better :
The landlady and Tam grew gracious,
Wi' favours, secret, sweet, and precious :
The Souter tauld his queerest stories ;
The landlord's laugh was ready chorus :
The storm without might rair and rustle,   *roar*
Tam did na mind the storm a whistle.

  Care, mad to see a man sae happy,
E'en drown'd himsel amang the nappy :
As bees flee hame wi' lades o' treasure,   *loads*
The minutes wing'd their way wi' pleasure :
Kings my be blest, but Tam was glorious,
O'er a' the ills o' life victorious !

  But pleasures are like poppies spread,
You seize the flow'r, its bloom is shed ;
Or like the snow falls in the river,
A moment white—then melts for ever ;
Or like the borealis race,
That flit ere you can point their place ;
Or like the rainbow's lovely form
Evanishing amid the storm.—
Nae man can tether time or tide ;
The hour approaches Tam maun ride ;
That hour, o' night's black arch the key-stane,
That dreary hour he mounts his beast in ;
And sic a night he taks the road in,
As ne'er poor sinner was abroad in.

  The wind blew as 'twad blawn its last ;   *would have*
The rattling showers rose on the blast ;
The speedy gleams the darkness swallow'd ;
Loud, deep, and lang, the thunder bellow'd :
That night, a child might understand,
The Deil had business on his hand.

  Weel mounted on his gray mare, Meg,
A better never lifted leg,
Tam skelpit on thro' dub and mire,   *dashed / puddle*
Despising wind, and rain, and fire ;
Whiles holding fast his gude blue bonnet ;   *Now*
Whiles crooning o'er some auld Scots sonnet ;   *song*
Whiles glowring round wi' prudent cares,   *staring*

As Tammie glowr'd, amaz'd and curious,
The mirth and fun grew fast and furious;

Lest bogles catch him unawares :
Kirk-Alloway was drawing nigh,
Whare ghaists and houlets nightly cry.—   owls

By this time he was cross the ford,
Whare, in the snaw, the chapman smoor'd ;   smothered
And past the birks and meikle stane,   birches ; big
Whare drunken Charlie brak's neck-bane ;
And thro' the whins, and by the cairn,   furze
Whare hunters fand the murder'd bairn :
And near the thorn, aboon the well,
Whare Mungo's mither hang'd hersel.—
Before him Doon pours all his floods ;
The doubling storm roars thro' the woods ;
The lightnings flash from pole to pole ;
Near and more near the thunders roll :
When, glimmering thro' the groaning trees,
Kirk-Alloway seem'd in a bleeze ;
Thro' ilka bore the beams were glancing ;   every cranny
And loud resounded mirth and dancing.—

Inspiring bold John Barleycorn !
What dangers thou canst make us scorn !
Wi' tippeny, we fear nae evil ;   ale
Wi' unsquabae, we'll face the devil !—   whisky
The swats sae ream'd in Tammie's noddle,
Fair play, he car'd na deils a boddle.   not ; farthing
But Maggie stood right sair astonish'd,
Till, by the heel and hand admonish'd,
She ventur'd forward on the light ;
And, vow ! Tam saw an unco sight !   woundrous

And scarcely had he Maggie rallied,
When out the hellish legion sallied.

Warlocks and witches in a dance ;
Nae cotillion, brent new frae France,
But hornpipes, jigs, strathspeys, and reels,
Put life and mettle in their heels.
A winnock-bunker in the east,   window-seat
There sat auld Nick, in shape o' beast ;
A towzie tyke, black, grim, and large,   shaggy dog
To gie them music was his charge :
He screw'd the pipes and gart them skirl,   made
Till roof and rafters a' did dirl.—   rattle
Coffins stood round, like open presses,
That shaw'd the dead in their last dresses ;
And by some devilish cantraip slight   weird trick
Each in its cauld hand held a light.—
By which heroic Tam was able
To note upon the haly table,
A murderer's banes in gibbet airns ;   irons
Twa span-lang, wee, unchristen'd bairns ;
A thief, new-cutted frae a rape,   rope
Wi' his last gasp his gab did gape ;   mouth
Five tomahawks, wi' blude red-rusted ;
Five scymitars, wi' murder crusted ;
A garter, which a babe had strangled ;
A knife, a father's throat had mangled,
Whom his ain son o' life bereft,
The grey hairs yet stack to the heft ;   stuck ; haft
Wi' mair o' horrible and aweful'
Which even to name wad be unlawful'.

stared	As Tammie glowr'd, amaz'd, and curious,	(A souple jade she was, and strang),	
	The mirth and fun grew fast and furious:	And how Tam stood, like ane bewitch'd,	
	The piper loud and louder blew;	And thought his very een enrich'd;	
	The dancers quick and quicker flew;	Even Satan glowr'd, and fidg'd fu' fain,	wriggled with delight
joined hands witch sweated and steamed rags tripped; shirt	They reel'd, they set, they cross'd, they cleekit,	And hotch'd and blew wi' might and main:	jerked
	Till ilka carlin swat and reekit,	Till first ae caper, syne anither,	then
	And coost her duddies to the wark,	Tam tint his reason a' thegither,	lost
	And linket at it in her sark !	And roars out, " Weel done, Cutty-sark ! "	

Now, Tam, O Tam! had thae been queans, — *these*
A' plump and strapping in their teens,
Their sarks, instead o' creeshie flannen, — *greasy*
Been snaw-white seventeen hunder linnen!
Thir breeks o' mine, my only pair, — *These*
That ance were plush, o' gude blue hair,
I wad hae gi'en them off my hurdies, — *buttocks*
For ae blink o' the bonie burdies! — *lasses*

But wither'd beldams, auld and droll,
Rigwoodie hags wad spean a foal, — *lean; wean*
Lowping and flinging on a crummock, — *leapfrog staff*
I wonder didna turn thy stomach.

But Tam kend what was what fu' brawlie, — *well*
There was ae winsome wench and wawlie, — *choice*
That night enlised in the core, — *company*
(Lang after kend on Carrick shore;
For mony a beast to dead she shot,
And perish'd mony a bony boat,
And shook baith meikle corn and bear, — *much; barley*
And kept the country-side in fear).
Her cutty sark, o' Paisley harn, — *short shift; coarse cloth*
That while a lassie she had worn,
In longitude tho' sorely scanty,
It was her best, and she was vauntie.— — *proud*
Ah ! little kend thy reverend grannie,
That sark she coft for her wee Nannie, — *bought*
Wi' twa pund Scots ('twas a' her riches),
Wad ever grac'd a dance of witches!

But here my Muse her wing maun cour; — *stoop*
Sic flights are far beyond her pow'r;
To sing how Nannie lap and flang, — *leaped and kicked*

And in an instant all was dark:
And scarcely had he Maggie rallied,
When out the hellish legion sallied.

As bees bizz out wi' angry fyke, — *fret*
When plundering herds assail their byke; — *shepherds; hive*
As open pussie's mortal foes, — *the hare's*
When, pop! she starts before their nose;
As eager runs the market-crowd,
When " Catch the thief ! " resounds aloud;
So Maggie runs, the witches follow,
Wi' mony an eldritch skreech and hollow. — *unearthly yell*

Ah, Tam ! Ah, Tam ! thou'll get thy fairin ! — *deserts*
In hell they'll roast thee like a herrin !
In vain thy Kate awaits thy comin !
Kate soon will be a woefu' woman !
Now, do thy speedy utmost, Meg,
And win the key-stane¹ of the brig;
There at them thou thy tail may toss,
A running stream they dare na cross.
But ere the key-stane she could make,
The fient a tail she had to shake ! — *devil*
For Nannie, far before the rest,
Hard upon noble Maggie prest,
And flew at Tam wi' furious ettle ; — *intent*
But little wist she Maggie's mettle—
Ae spring brought off her master hale, — *whole*
But left behind her ain grey tail :
The carlin claught her by the rump, — *clutched*
And left poor Maggie scarce a stump.

Now, wha this tale o' truth shall read,
Ilk man and mother's son, take heed :
Whene'er to drink you are inclin'd,
Or cutty-sarks run in your mind,
Think, ye may buy the joys o'er dear,
Remember Tam o' Shanter's mare.

The carlin caught her by the rump,
And left poor Maggie scarce a stump.

The Haggis Feast at Poosie Mansies Inn, Mauchline; by Alexander Carse

*Fair fa' your honest, sonsie face,
Great Chieftain o' the Puddin-race!*

To A Haggis

<table>
<tr><td>jolly</td><td>Fair, fa' your honest, sonsie face,
Great Chieftain o' the Puddin-race !
Aboon them a' ye tak your place,</td></tr>
<tr><td>Paunch;
small guts
worthy</td><td>Painch, tripe, or thairm :
Weel are ye wordy of a grace
As lang's my arm.</td></tr>
</table>

buttocks The groaning trencher there ye fill,
Your hurdies like a distant hill,
Your pin wad help to mend a mill
In time o' need,
While thro' your pores the dews distil
Like amber bead.

clean His knife see Rustic-labor dight,
skill An' cut you up wi' ready slight,
Trenching your gushing entrails bright
Like onie ditch ;
And then, O what a glorious sight,
-smoking Warm-reekin, rich !

horn-spoon Then, horn for horn they stretch an' strive,
Deil tak the hindmost, on they drive,
well-swelled
stomachs Till a' their weel-swall'd kytes belyve
by-and-bys Are bent like drums ;
almost ;
burst Then auld Guidman, maist like to rive,
Bethankit hums.

surfeit Is there that owre his French *ragout*,
Or *olio* that wad staw a sow,
Or *fricassee* wad mak her spew
disgust Wi' perfect sconner,
Looks down wi' sneering, scornful' view
On sic a dinner ?

Poor devil ! see him owre his trash,
feeble ; rush As feckless as a wither'd rash,
His spindle shank a guid whip-lash,
first ; nut His nieve a nit ;
Thro' bluidy flood or field to dash,
O how unfit !

But mark the Rustic, haggis-fed,
The trembling earth resounds his tread,
ample Clap in his walie nieve a blade,
He'll mak it whissle ;
top off An' legs, an' arms, an' heads will sned,
tops of
thistle Like taps o' thrissle.

Ye Pow'rs wha mak mankind your care,
And dish them out their bill o' fare,
watery Auld Scotland wants nae skinking ware,
splashes ;
wooden That jaups in luggies ;
porringers But, if ye wish her gratefu' prayer,
Gie her a Haggis !

One of the unique ceremonies at any Burns Supper is The Address to the Haggis. The piper leads the chef into the room, and the haggis is toasted. Following this, the poem is recited with highly theatrical gestures as the knife is plunged into the haggis.

*The best-laid schemes o' Mice an' Men
Gang aft a-gley.*

To A Mouse

ON TURNING HER UP IN HER NEST, WITH THE PLOUGH,
NOVEMBER 1785

    WEE, sleekit, cowrin, tim'rous beastie,
    O, what a panic's in thy breastie !
    Thou need na start awa sae hasty,
                Wi' bickering brattle !   *hasty scamper*
    I wad be laith to rin an' chase thee,   *loath*
                Wi' murd'ring pattle !   *plough-staff*

    I'm truly sorry Man's dominion
    Has broken Nature's social union,
    An' justifies that ill opinion,
                Which makes thee startle,
    At me, thy poor, earth-born companion,
                An' fellow-mortal !

    I doubt na, whyles, but thou may thieve ;   *sometimes*
    What then ? poor beastie, thou maun live !
    A daimen icker in a thrave   *odd ear; twenty-four sheaves*
                'S a sma' request.
    I'll get a blessin wi' the lave,   *what's left*
                An' never miss't !

    Thy wee-bit housie, too, in ruin !
    Its silly wa's the win's are strewin !   *feeble*
    An' naething, now, to big a new ane,   *build*
                O' foggage green !   *moss*
    An' bleak December's winds ensuin,
                Baith snell an' keen !

    Thou saw the fields laid bare an' waste,
    An' weary Winter comin fast,
    An' cozie here, beneath the blast,
                Thou thought to dwell,
    Till crash ! the cruel coulter past
                Out thro' thy cell.

    That wee-bit heap o' leaves an' stibble   *stubble*
    Has cost thee monie a weary nibble !
    Now thou's turn'd out, for a' thy trouble,
                But house or hald,   *Without; holding*
    To thole the Winter's sleety dribble,   *endure*
                An' cranreuch cauld !   *hoar-frost*

    But, Mousie, thou art no thy lane,   *alone*
    In proving foresight may be vain :
    The best-laid schemes o' Mice an' Men
                Gang aft a-gley,   *awry*
    An' lea'e us nought but grief an' pain,
                For promis'd joy !

    Still thou art blest, compar'd wi' me !
    The present only toucheth thee :
    But, Och ! I backward cast my e'e
                On prospects drear !
    An' forward, tho' I canna see,
                I guess an' fear !

*Just as the world of the mouse literally and figuratively collapsed, the world of
Burns had gang aft a-gley, as he considered a one-way passage to Jamaica.*

While round the fire the hav'rels keckle
To see me loup;

Address To The Tooth-ache

(Written by the Author at a time when he was grievously tormented by that Disorder.)

sting	My curse on your envenom'd stang,
	That shoots my tortur'd gums alang,
ear	An' thro' my lugs gies mony a bang
	Wi' gnawin vengeance ;
	Tearing my nerves wi' bitter twang,
	Like racking engines.

A' down my beard the slavers trickle,

big / half-wits chuckle / leap / swear ; heckling-comb / backside

I cast the wee stools owre the meikle,
While round the fire the hav'rels keckle,
To see me loup;
I curse an' ban, an' wish a heckle
Were i' their doup.

Whan fevers burn, or agues freeze us,
Rheumatics gnaw, or colics squeeze us,
Our neebors sympathize, to ease us,
Wi' pitying moan ;
But thou—the hell o' a' diseases,
They mock our groan.

woes / Bad harvests ; foolish	O' a' the num'rous human dools,
	Ill hairsts, daft bargains, cutty-stools,
repetentance-mould	Or worthy friends laid i' the mools,
	Sad sight to see !
annoyance	The tricks o' knaves, or fash o' fools,
first place	Thou bear'st the gree.

Whare'er that place be, priests ca' hell,
Whar a' the tones o' mis'ry's yell,
An' plagues in ranked numbers tell
row   In deadly raw,
Thou, Tooth-ache, surely bear'st the bell
Aboon them a' !

fellow   O ! thou grim mischief-makin chiel,
makes   That gars the notes o' discord squeel,
Till human-kind aft dances a reel
In gore a shoe thick,
Give ; foes   Gie a' the faes o' Scotland's weal
twelve-month's   A townmond's tooth-ache !

Another example of Burns expressing everyday feelings – such as the intense pain of a toothache – which are familiar to all. But not forgetting to perceive the slightly perverted sense of humour of the onlookers.

The Cotter's Saturday Night

At length his lonely Cot appears in view,
Beneath the shelter of an aged tree;

Th' expectant wee-things, toddlin, stacher through
To meet their Dad, wi' flichterin noise and glee.

*His clean hearth-stane, his thrifty, Wifie's smile
The lisping infant, prattling on his knee,*

THE COTTER'S SATURDAY NIGHT
INSCRIBED TO R. AITKEN, ESQ.

*Let not Ambition mock their useful toil,
Their homely joys and destiny obscure ;
Nor Grandeur hear, with a disdainful smile,
The short but simple annals of the Poor.*
            GRAY

I

My lov'd, my honor'd, much respected friend!
   No mercenary Bard his homage pays ;
With honest pride, I scorn each selfish end,
   My dearest meed, a friend's esteem and praise :
To you I sing, in simple Scottish lays,
   The lowly train in life's sequester'd scene ;
   The native feelings strong, the guileless ways,
What Aiken in a Cottage would have been ;
Ah ! tho' his worth unknown, far happier there, I ween !

II

November chill blaws loud wi' angry sugh ;
   The short'ning winter-day is near a close ;
The miry beasts retreating frae the pleugh ;
   The black'ning trains o' craws to their repose :
   The toil-worn Cotter frae his labor goes,
This night his weekly moil is at an end,
   Collects his spades, his mattocks, and his hoes,
Hoping the morn in ease and rest to spend,
And weary o'er the moor, his course does hameward ward bend.

III

At length his lonely Cot appears in view,
   Beneath the shelter of an aged tree ;
Th' expectant wee-things, toddlin, stacher through *totter*
   To meet their Dad, wi' flichterin noise and glee. *fluttering*
   His wee-bit ingle, blinkin bonilie,
His clean hearth-stane, his thrifty Wifie's smile,
   The lisping infant, prattling on his knee,
Does a' his weary carking cares beguile,
And makes him quite forget his labor and his toil.

IV

Belyve, the elder bairns come drapping in, *By-and-by*
   At service out, amang the Farmers roun' ;
Some ca' the pleugh, some herd, some tentie rin *drive ; heedful run*
   A cannie errand to a neebor town : *easy*
   Their eldest hope, their Jenny, woman grown,
In youthfu' bloom, Love sparkling in her e'e,
   Comes hame, perhaps, to shew a braw new gown,
Or deposite her sair-won penny-fee, *hard-; wages*
To help her Parents dear, if they in hardship be.

V

With joy unfeign'd, brothers and sisters meet,
   And each for other's, weelfare kindly spiers : *asks*
The social hours, swift-wing'd, unnotic'd fleet ;
   Each tells the uncos that he sees or hears. *uncommon things*
   The Parents, partial, eye their hopeful years ;
Anticipation forward points the view ;
   The Mother, wi' her needle and her sheers,
Gars auld claes look amaist as weel's the new ; *Makes ; clothes ; almost*
The Father mixes a' wi' admonition due.

This poem is symbolic of 18th century rural Christian values. Overly sentimental for some, Burns nevertheless eloquently empathises with a rural family not dissimilar to his own family upbringing with its stern Calvinist roots and local language.

VI

Their Master's and their Mistress's command,
    The youngkers a' are warned to obey ;
And mind their labors wi' an eydent hand, *diligent*
    And ne'er, tho' out o' sight, to jauk or play : *idle*
    ' And O ! be sure to fear the Lord alway !
' And mind you duty, duely, morn and night !
    ' Lest in temptation's path ye gang astray,
' Implore his counsel and assisting might :
    They never sought in vain that sought the Lord
        aright.'

VII

But hark ! a rap comes gently to the door ;
    Jenny, wha kens the meaning o' the same,
Tells how a neebor lad cam o'er the moor,
    To do some errands, and convoy her hame.
    The wily Mother sees the conscious flame
Sparkle in Jenny's e'e, and flush her cheek,
    With heart-struck, anxious care, enquires his name,
While Jenny hafflins is afraid to speak ; *half*
Weel pleas'd the Mother hears, it's nae wild, worth-
        less Rake.

VIII

With kindly welcome, Jenny brings him ben ; *in*
    A strappan youth, he takes the Mother's eye ;
Blythe Jenny sees the visit's no ill taen ;
    The Father cracks of horses, pleughs, and kye. *chats ; cattle*
    The Youngster's artless heart o'erflows wi' joy,
But blate and laithfu', scarce can weel behave ; *shy ; sheepish*
    The Mother, wi' a woman's wiles, can spy
What makes the Youth sae bashfu' and sae grave ;
Weel-pleas'd to think her bairn's respected like the
        lave. *rest*

IX

O happy love ! where love like this is found !
    O heart-felt raptures ! bliss beyond compare !
I've paced much this weary, mortal round,
    And sage Experience bids me this declare—
    ' If Heaven a draught of heavenly pleasure spare,
' One cordial in this melancholy Vale,
    ' 'Tis when a youthful, loving, modest Pair,
' In other's arms, breathe out the tender tale,
' Beneath the milk-white thorn that scents
        the ev'ning gale.'

X

Is there, in human form, that bears a heart—
    A Wretch ! a Villain ! lost to love and truth !
That can, with studied, sly, ensnaring art,
    Betray sweet Jenny's unsuspecting youth ?
    Curse on his perjur'd arts ! dissembling smooth !
Are Honor, Virtue, Conscience, all exil'd ?
    Is there no Pity, no relenting Ruth,
Points to the Parents fondling o'er their Child ?
Then paints the ruin'd Maid, and their distraction
        wild !

XI

But now the Supper crows their simple board,
    The healsome Parritch, chief of Scotia's food : *wholesome*
The soupe their only Hawkie does afford, *sup ; cow*
    That 'yont the hallan snugly chows her cood : *beyond ; partition*
    The Dame brings forth, in complimental mood,
To grace the lad, her weel-hain'd kebbuck, fell, *-saved cheese, strong*
    And aft he's prest, and aft he ca's it guid ;
The frugal Wifie, garrulous, will tell,
How 'twas a towmond auld, sin' Lint was i' the *twelve-month ; flax flower*
        bell.

The Mother, wi' her needle and her sheers,
Gars auld claes look amaist as weel's the new;

With kindly welcome, Jenny brings him ben;
A strappan youth, he takes the Mother's eye;

XII

The cheerfu' Supper done, wi' serious face,
    They, round the ingle, form a circle wide ;
The Sire turns o'er, wi' patriarchal grace,
hall-   The big ha'-Bible, ance his Father's pride :
    His bonnet rev'rently is laid aside,
grey side-locks His lyart haffets wearing thin and bare ;
    Those strains that once did sweet in Zion glide,
chooses   He wales a portion with judicious care ;
'And let us worship God ! ' he says, with solemn air.

XIII

They chant their artless notes in simple guise ;
    They tune their hearts, by far the noblest aim :
Perhaps *Dundee's* wild-warbling measures rise,
    Or plaintive *Martyrs*, worthy of the name ;
feeds   Or noble *Elgin* beets the heaven-ward flame,
The sweetest far of Scotia's holy lays :
    Compar'd with these, Italian trills are tame ;
The tickl'd ears no heart-felt raptures raise ;
Nae unison hae they, with our Creator's praise.

XIV

The priest-like Father reads the sacred page,
    How Abram was the Friend of God on high ;
Or, Moses bade eternal warfare wage
    With Amalek's ungracious progeny ;
    Or how the royal Bard did groaning lye,
Beneath the stroke of Heaven's avenging ire ;
    Or Job's pathetic plaint, and wailing cry ;
Or rapt Isaiah's wild, seraphic fire ;
Or rather Holy Seers that tune the sacred lyre.

XV

Perhaps the Christian Volume is the theme,
    How guiltless blood for guilty man was shed ;
How He, who bore in heaven the second name,
    Had not on Earth whereon to lay His head ;
    How His first followers and servants sped ;
The precepts sage they wrote to many a land :
    How he, who lone in Patmos banished,
Saw in the sun a mighty angel stand ;
And heard great Bab'lon's doom pronounc'd by Heaven's command.

XVI

Then kneeling down to Heaven's Eternal King,
    The Saint, the Father, and the Husband prays :
Hope ' springs exulting on triumphant wing,' [1]
    That thus they all shall meet in future days :
    There, ever bask in uncreated rays,
No more to sigh, or shed the bitter tear,
    Together hymning their Creator's praise,
In such society, yet still more dear ;
While circling Time moves round in an eternal sphere.

XVII

Compar'd with this, how poor Religion's pride,
    In all the pomp of method, and of art,
When men display to congregations wide,
    Devotion's ev'ry grace, except the heart !
    The Power, incens'd, the Pageant will desert,
The pompous strain, the sacerdotal stole ;
    But haply, in some Cottage far apart,
May hear, well-pleas'd, the language of the Soul ;
And in His Book of Life the Inmates poor enroll.

XVIII

Then homeward all take off their sev'eral way ;
  The youngling Cottagers retire to rest :
The Parent-pair their secret homage pay,
  And proffer up to Heaven the warm request.
  That He who stills the raven's clam'rous nest,
And decks the lily fair in flow'ry pride,
  Would, in the way His Wisdom sees the best,
For them and for their little ones provide ;
But chiefly, in their hearts with Grace divine preside.

XIX

From scenes like these, old Scotia's grandeur springs,
  That makes her lov'd at home, rever'd abroad ;
Princes and lords are but the breath of kings,
  ' An honest man's the noblest work of God :'
  And certes, in fair Virtue's heavenly road,
The Cottage leaves the Palace far behind ;
  What is a lordling's pomp ! a cumbrous load,
Disguising oft the wretch of human kind,
Studied in arts of Hell, in wickedness refin'd !

XX

O Scotia ! my dear, my native soil !
  From whom my warmest wish to Heaven is sent !
Long may thy hardy sons of rustic toil
  Be blest with health, and peace, and sweet content !
  And, O ! may Heaven their simple lives prevent
From Luxury's contagion, weak and vile !
  Then, howe'er crowns and coronets be rent,
A virtuous Populace may rise the while,
And stand a wall of fire around their much-lov'd Isle.

XXI

O Thou ! who pour'd the patriotic tide,
  That stream'd thro' Wallace's undaunted heart ;
Who dare'd to, nobly, stem tyrannic pride,
  Or nobly die, the second glorious part,
  (The Patriot's God, peculiarly thou art,
  His friend, inspirer, guardian, and reward !)
  O never, never, Scotia's realm desert,
But still the Patriot, and the Patriot-Bard,
In bright succession raise, her Ornament and Guard !

The Sire turns o'er, wi' patriarchal grace,
The big ha'-Bible, ance his Father's pride:

Songs by Rob' Burns

*But blessings on your frosty pow,
John Anderson my jo.*

John Anderson My Jo

dear	JOHN ANDERSON my jo, John,
acquainted	When we were first Acquent ;
	Your locks were like the raven,
smooth	Your bony brow was brent ;
bald	But now your brow is beld, John,
	Your locks are like the snaw ;
head	But blessings on your frosty pow,
	John Anderson my Jo.

John Anderson my jo, John,
    We clamb the hill the gither ; *(together)*
And mony a canty day John, *(cheerful)*
    We've had wi' ane anither :
Now we maun totter down, John,
    And hand in hand we'll go ;
And sleep the gither at the foot,
    John Anderson my Jo.

Nostalgia probably accounts for the popularity of this poem. According to Burns it refers to no particular person. However the song's widespread appeal is best indicated by the frequency with which it was illustrated by 19th century artists.

*Gin a body meet a body
Comin' thr' the rye*

Comin Thro' The Rye

draggled	Comin thro' the rye, poor body, Comin thro' the rye, She draigl't a' her petticoatie Comin thro' the rye.
wet ; creature	*Oh Jenny's a' weet, poor body, Jenny's seldom dry, She draigl't a' her petticoatie Comin thro' the rye.*
Should	Gin a body met a body Comin thro' the rye, Gin a body kiss a body, Need a body cry !
	Gin a body meet a body Comin thro' the glen ; Gin a body kiss a body, Need the warld ken !

Although Burns contributed few lines to this well-known ditty, undoubtedly he would have concurred with the sentiments of the ballad.

Now's the day, and now's the hour;
See the front o' battle lour;

Scots, Wha Hae

Ode — Bruce's address to his troops at Bannockburn — Tune Lewis Gordon.

Scots, wha hae wi' Wallace bled,
Scots wham Bruce has aften led,
Welcome to your gory bed
  Or to glorious victorie!

Now's the day, & now's the hour
See the front o' battle lour;
  See approach proud Edward's power
  Edward! Chains & Slaverie!

Wha will be a traitor-knave?
Wha can fill a coward's grave?
Wha sae base as be a slave?
  Traitor! Coward! turn & flee!
Wha for Scotland's king & law
Freedom's sword will strongly draw,
Free-man stand, or Free-man fa'
  Caledonian! on wi' me!

By Oppression's woes & pains
By your sons in servile chains
We will drain our dearest veins
  But they shall they shall be free!
Lay the proud usurpers low!
Tyrants fall in every foe!
Liberty's in every blow!
  Forward! let us do, or die!!!

Burns the patriot issued a clarion call to all Scots based on an address that Robert the Bruce might have made to his troops on the morning of their conquest of the English at Bannockburn. The Lewis Gordon tune was later replaced by Hey Tuttie Tattie, possibly Bruce's original marching tune. The strident style of Burns handwriting left no doubt about the depth of his passion, with the closing lyrics being penned with a flourish.

Bannockburn

Flow gently, sweet Afton among thy green braes,
Flow gently, I'll sing thee a song in thy praise:

Flow Gently, Sweet Afton

<small>hills</small>   Flow gently, sweet Afton, among thy green braes,
        Flow gently, I'll sing thee a song in thy praise ;
    My Mary's asleep by thy murmuring stream,
        Flow gently, sweet Afton, disturb not her dream!

    Thou stock dove whose echo resounds thro' the glen,
<small>ravine</small>   Ye wild whistling blackbirds in yon thorny den,
    Thou green-crested lapwing, thy screaming forbear,
        I charge you, disturb not my slumbering fair !

    How lofty, sweet Afton, thy neighbouring hills,
        Far mark'd with the courses of clear, winding rills ;
    There daily I wander, as noon rises high,
        My flocks and my Mary's sweet cot in my eye

    How pleasant thy banks and green vallies below,
        Where wild in the woodlands the primroses blow ;
    There oft, as mild Ev'ning weeps over the lea,
        The sweet-scented birk shades my Mary and me.

    Thy crystal stream, Afton, how lovely it glides,
        And winds by the cot where my Mary resides ;
    How wanton thy waters her snowy feet lave,
        As, gathering sweet flowerets, she stems thy clear wave.

    Flow gently sweet Afton, among thy green braes,
        Flow gently, sweet river, the theme of my lays ;
    My Mary's asleep by thy murmuring stream,
        Flow gently, sweet Afton, disturb not her dream !

Throughout the flowing lyrics, which so beautifully complement the movement of the Afton Water, are references to Mary. This is not believed to be Highland Mary, who is thought to be buried many miles away.

*Ye Banks and braes o' bonie Doon,
How can ye bloom sae fresh and fair:*

The Banks O' Doon

Y<small>E</small> Banks and braes o' bonie Doon,
    How can ye bloom sae fresh and fair ;
How can ye chant, ye little birds,
    And I sae weary fu' o' care !
Thou'll break my heart thou warbling bird,
    That wantons thro' the flowering thorn :
Thou minds me o' departed joys,
    Departed never to return.

    every

    stole

Oft hae I rov'd by bonie Doon,
    To see the rose and woodbine twine ;
And ilka bird sang o' its luve,
    And fondly sae did I o' mine.
Wi' lightsome heart I pu'd a rose,
    Fu' sweet upon its thorny tree ;
And my fause luver staw my rose,
    But, ah ! he left the thorn wi' me.

Written for Johnson's Scots Musical Museum by Burns, this poem concerned young Peggy Kennedy, known to Burns, but betrothed to Andrew McDowall, who abandoned her for another, also from a wealthy family.

Brig o' Doon; Spanning the Doon.

*Gie fools their silks and knaves their wine,
A man's a man for a' that:*

For A' That And A' That

Is there, for honesty poverty
   That hangs his head, and a' that;
The coward-slave, we pass him by,
   We dare be poor for a' that!
For a' that, and a' that,
   Ours toils obscure, and a' that,
The rank is but the guinea's stamp,
   The man's the gowd for a' that. *gold*

What though on hamely fare we dine,
   Wear hoddin grey, and a' that; *coarse grey woollen*
Gie fools their silks, and knaves their wine,
   A man's a man for a' that:
For a' that, and a' that,
   Their tinsel show, and a' that;
The honest man, though e'er sae poor,
   Is king o' men for a' that.

Ye see yon birkie, ca'd a lord, *fellow; called*
   Wha struts, and stares, and a' that;
Though hundreds worship at his word,
   He's but a coof for a' that: *fool*

For a' that, and a' that,
   His ribband, star, and a' that,
The man of independent mind,
   He looks and laughs at a' that.

A prince can mak a belted knight,
   A marquis, duke, and a' that;
But an honest man's aboon his might, *above*
   Gude faith, he mauna fa' that! *must not try*
For a' that, and a' that,
   Their dignities, and a' that,
The pith o' sense, and pride o' worth,
   Are higher ranks than a' that.

Then let us pray that come it may,
   As come it will for a' that,
That sense and worth, o'er a' the earth,
   May bear the gree, and a' that. *have the first place*
For a' that, and a' that,
   Its comin yet for a' that,
That man to man, the warld o'er,
   Shall brothers be for a' that.

Robert Burns was now deeply affected by the cause of the French Revolution, which espoused the brotherhood of man, a belief close to his heart. Not for the first time, liberal thoughts landed Burns in difficulty. The lyrics to this song placed his job with the excise in jeopardy.

*We'll tak a cup o' kindness yet
For auld lang syne.*

Auld Lang Syne

SHOULD auld acquaintance be forgot
  And never brought to mind?
Should auld acquaintance be forgot,
  And auld lang syne!

*For auld lang syne, my dear,
  For auld lang syne,
We'll tak a cup o' kindness yet
  For auld lang syne.*

And surely ye'll be your pint stowp!   *pay for; stoup*
  And surely I'll be mine!
And we'll tak a cup o' kindess yet,
  For auld lang syne.

We twa hae run about the braes,
  And pou'd the gowans fine;   *pulled*
But we've wander'd mony a weary fitt,   *foot*
  Sin auld lang syne.   *Since*

We twa hae paidl'd in the burn,   *waded*
  Frae morning sun till dine;   *noon*
But seas between us braid hae roar'd,   *broad*
  Sin auld lang syne.

And there's a hand, my trusty fiere!   *companion*
  And gie's a hand o' thine!   *give me*
And we' tak a right gude-willie waught,   *hearty draught*
  For auld lang syne.

Throughout the year hands of friendship are extended by millions of friends interlocking hands and singing Auld Lang Syne. At Hogmanay the ritual is followed by many more millions. Robert Burns, responsible for some of the lyrics, would have been proud.

Burns Supper, Edinburgh, 18..

BURN.

NEW YORK.—The Burns Centenary celebration in this city was auspiciously commenced on Monday evening with an oration by the Rev. Henry Ward Beecher in the Cooper Institute. There were three thousand people present, and among the audience were several of the most prominent citizens of New York.

1859

MONTREAL.—About seven o'clock in the evening the City Concert Hall, which was beautifully and appropriately decorated for the occasion with illustrations of and quotations from the works of Burns, under the direction and auspices of the Montreal Burns Club, was filled with an assemblage as brilliant, perhaps, as any that ever met within its walls. Shortly after 7 o'clock the Chairman (the Hon. John Rose) and the other speakers entered amid applause, and took their seats on the platform.

Perhaps one of the most remarkable features of the evening was a telegraphic apparatus on the platform, with wires running along the hall, and connecting with those in the street, by which, during the night, sentiments were exchanged with, and received from, other assemblies of the same kind, in Canada and the States.

1859

MELBOURNE.—This festival was celebrated on Tuesday in the Exhibition Building. The banqueters numbered not fewer than 600 gentlemen, who were seated at several rows of tables, arranged in the centre of the hall, clear of wings. The galleries were occupied by a number of ladies.

A BURNS DINNER IN SOUTH AMERICA.—The St Andrews Society of the River Plate held a Burns anniversary dinner in Buenos Ayres with great success. About 125 gentlemen marched into the Concordia Hall, headed by a piper, and sat down to dinner. The "Memory of Burns" was proposed in orthodox fashion, and all the toasts were drank in real "mountain dew."

Monumental Bust of Burns in Westminster Abbey

A Monumental Bust of the Scottish National Poet Robert Burns, the cost of which has been provided by Subscriptions of not more than One Shilling each, contributed by his Countrymen and Admirers all over the world, will be Unveiled on Saturday the 7th March, at 4 o'clock afternoon, in the Poets' Corner, Westminster Abbey, by the Right Hon: the Earl of Rosebery.

The Executive Committee of Subscribers, by the kind permission of the Very Rev the Dean of Westminster, request the favour of the Company of *Preceptor Wilson* in the Jerusalem Chamber, Westminster Abbey, at 3·45 previous to the Ceremony of Unveiling in the Abbey.

In name of the Committee,

Glasgow, 26th February, 1885.

William Wilson, Chairman
George Jackson, Secretary

An early Reply addressed to the Secretary, 122 Buchanan Street, Glasgow, will oblige.

Note.—THIS CARD REQUIRES TO BE PRESENTED ON ENTERING.

Centenary procession, Dumfries.

AT a MEETING of some Friends and Admirers of the late Scottish Bard, ROBERT BURNS, assembled [at] the George Inn, for the purpose of taking into consideration [the] measure of opening a public Subscription for erecting a [Ma]usoleum over his remains in St. Michael's Church-yard, [Du]mfries. 1814

ANA

Вслѣдъ за отцомъ, полчасомъ лишь позднѣе,
И сыновья приходятъ изъ села:
Одинъ пахать; другой, посмышленнѣе,
На ярмаркѣ улаживалъ дѣла.

[The] above verse from the Cotter's Saturday Night [was] translated into Russian by V. Kostomaroff and [the] Russian-English version is shown below and can [be] compared with the original verse underneath.

[B]ehind the father, scarcely half-an-hour later,
[T]he sons come from the village.
[T]he one has been at the plough, the other cleverly
[D]id his business at the fair.

[Be]lyve, the elder bairns come drapping in,
 At service out, amang the farmers roun';
[So]me ca' the pleugh, some herd, some tentie rin
 A cannie errand to a neebor town:

IMPORTANT RELICS OF BURNS.

[The]re will be Sold, by Public Roup, within the TAM O' SHANTER [I]NN, High Street, Ayr, upon THURSDAY, the 30th day of July [ne]xt, at Two o'clock afternoon,
[T]HE CHAIRS which were used by "TAM O' SHANTER," and [by] "SOUTER JOHNNY," as also the famed STIRRUP CUP; [tog]ether with a LETTER addressed to the Honourable Henry [Ers]kine, Dean of Faculty, Edinburgh, holograph of the Poet. [The]se relics will be disposed of separately. With regard [the]reto further information may be had on application to Messrs [—— &] D. FERGUSSON, Solicitors, Ayr, Agents for the Trustees of [the] late Mr Andrew Glass, who acquired these relics at con[sid]erable expense many years ago.

ROBERT DEWAR, Auctioneer.

[A]yr, 8th July, 1885.

BURNS AND THE GENTLEMAN'S LIBRARY.

Burns was one day in a gentleman's library. The collection was very fine, but the owner happened to be unable to appreciate the contents. After some conversation with Burns, he said he liked to see books with a handsome exterior. Next morning the poet was found to have left the following couplet on the library table:—

Free through these books, ye maggots, make
 your winding;
But, for the owner's sake, oh, spare the binding.

"MOURNINGS."

No man could more severely inflict the castigation of reproof than Burns. The following anecdote will illustrate this fact. The conversation one night at the King's Arms Inn, Dumfries, turning on the death of a townsman, whose funeral was to take place on the following day. "By-the-bye," said one of the company, addressing himself to Burns, "I wish you would lend me your black coat for the occasion, my own being rather out of repair." "Having myself to attend the same funeral," answered Burns, "I am sorry that I cannot lend you my *sables*; but I can recommend a most excellent substitute; *throw your character over your shoulders*—that will be the *blackest* coat you ever wore in your lifetime."

54　　　　PUNCH, OR THE LONDON CHARIVARI.　　　[FEBRUARY 5, 1859.

GRAND BURNS' FESTIVAL. BROWN ENTERTAINS HIS FRIEND WI A HAGGIS!

An idyllic romance between Highland Mary (Mary Campbell) and Rober Burns was shattered by pregnancy, a bigamy charge, and most tragically the death of Mary.

Acknowledgements:

The publisher wishes to thank all those who assisted in the publication of this book including the pictorial material acknowledged here: fc (port), Mitchell Library, Glasgow; 1, Mitchell Library, Glasgow; 14 (top), Trustees, Burns Cottage & Museum; 6 (br), by courtesy Edinburgh City Libraries; 7 (br), by courtesy Edinburgh City Libraries; 15 Edinburgh District Council Museums and Art Galleries; Mitchell Library, Glasgow, pp 17-31 (incl) with exception of pp 22 and 24. Unless indicated all other illustrations property of publisher.